150
First Spanish
Phrases

Angela Wilkes

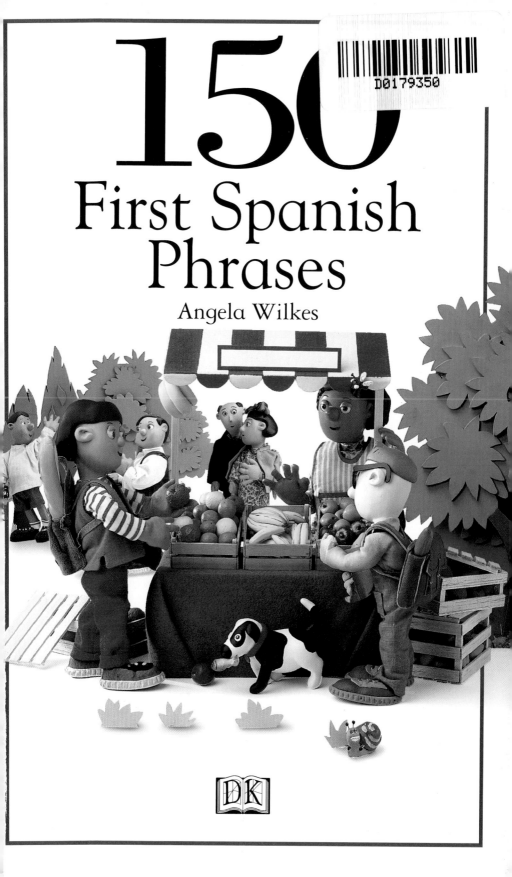

DK

How to use this book

Hi! I'm Emma.

In this book, **Emma, Eddie,** and **Erin** help you learn everyday Spanish! They teach you 150 phrases that are easy to say. You can use the phrases when you are traveling in Spanish-speaking countries. Here you can find out how to use the book.

The heading
The title and introduction tell you about the subject of the page.

Shopping for food

Here and on the next page you can learn how to ask for things and find out how much they cost.

61 Four oranges.
Cuatro naranjas.

62 A kilo of apples, please.
Un kilo de manzanas, por favor.

KWAH-troe nah-RAHN-hahs.

Oon KEE-loe deh mahn-ZAH-nahs, pohr fah-VOHR.

63 How much is it?
¿Cuánto es?

64 Ten pesetas fifty centavos.
Diez pesetas con cincuenta centavos.

¡KWAHN-toe ehs?

Dee-EZ peh-SEH-tahs kohn seen-KWEHN-tah cehn-TAH-voce.

20

Color-coded contents
The book covers 12 main subjects. They are color-coded for easy reference by tabs on the side of each page. You will find the key to the tabs on the front jacket flap.

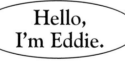

Hello, I'm Eddie.

Phrases
Each phrase is numbered and given in English first. A speech bubble then gives you the phrase in Spanish.

Pronunciation guide
Beneath the picture is a pronunciation guide showing how to say the Spanish phrase. Practice reading the phrase out loud so that you know what it should sound like.

Ten useful phrases

Ten of the most useful phrases in the book are listed on the back jacket flap so that you can find them quickly.

Everyday situations
The book gives you Spanish phrases to use in all sorts of situations. Always be polite when you are speaking to people and remember to say please.

Hidden friends

As you learn the phrases, see if you can spot Felix Fly, Cyril the Dog, and Sebastian Snail getting in to trouble.

Word list
Many subjects are followed by an illustrated word list that gives you extra vocabulary. You can use words from the word list to vary the phrases.

Looking words up

If you want to find a particular word or phrase quickly, look it up in the index. English words are listed in the front of the index and Spanish words at the back.

Hello, I'm Erin.

First words

Here are some words and phrases you will need in everyday situations.

1 Hello!

¡Hola!

¡OH-lah!

2 Good morning.

Buenos días.

BWEH-noce DEE-ahs.

3 Good evening.

Buenas tardes.

BWEH-nahs TAHR-dehs.

4 Good-bye.

Adiós.

Ah-dee-OCE.

5 Good night.

Buenas noches.

BWEH-nahs NOE-chehs.

6 Yes.
Sí.

See.

7 No.
No.

Noe.

8 Please.
Por favor.

Pohr fah-VOHR.

9 Thank you.
Gracias.

GRAH-see-ahs.

10 Excuse me.
Disculpe.

Dees-KOOL-peh.

11 Sorry.
Lo siento.

Loe see-EHN-toe.

Helpful phrases

Here are some more phrases that you will
find useful when you start to speak Spanish.

12 How are things?

¿Cómo estás?

¿KOH-moe ehs-TAHS?

13 Fine, thanks.

Bien, gracias.

Bee-EHN, GRAH-see-ahs.

14 See you.

Nos vemos.

Noce VEH-moce.

15 Do you speak English?

¿Habla inglés?

¿AH-blah een-GLEHS?

16 A little.

Un poco.

Oon POE-koe.

17 I don't speak Spanish.

No hablo español.

Noe AH-bloe ehs-pah-NYOHL.

18 More slowly, please.

Más despacio, por favor.

Mahs dehs-PAH-see-oh, pohr fah-VOHR.

19 I don't understand.

No entiendo.

Noe ehn-tee-EHN-doe.

20 Can you repeat that, please?

¿Puede repetir eso, por favor?

¿PWEH-deh reh-peh-TEER EH-soe, pohr fah-VOHR?

7

Finding the way

Here and on the next page you can find out
how to ask for simple directions.

21 Excuse me, where's the Café Flora?

> Disculpe,
> ¿dónde es el
> Café Flora?

Dees-KOOL-peh, ¿DOHN-deh ehs ehl Kah-FEH FLOH-rah?

22 It's over there

> Es por
> allá

Ehs pohr ah-YAH

23 ... opposite the cathedral.

> ... frente a
> la catedral.

*... FREHN-teh ah lah
kah-teh-DRAHL.*

24 Where are the stores?

¿Dónde están los almacenes?

¿DOHN-deh ehs-TAHN loce ahl-mah-SEH-nehs?

25 They are in Church Street.

Están en Church Street.

Ehs-TAHN ehn Church Street.

26 Is that far?

¿Es lejos?

¿Ehs LEH-hoce?

27 About five minutes walking.

A unos cinco minutos a pie.

Ah OO-noce SEEN-koh mee-NOO-toce ah pee-eh.

28 Is there a supermarket near here?

¿Hay un supermercado cerca de aquí?

¿Ah-ee oon soo-pehr-mehr-KAH-doe SEHR-kah deh ah-KEE?

29 Yes, just next to the bank.

Sí, junto al banco.

See, HUHN-toe ahl BAHN-koe.

Word list

information
información
een-fohr-mah-see-OHN

market
mercado
mehr-KAH-doe

airport
aeropuerto
ah-eh-roh-PWEHR-toe

hotel
hotel
oh-TEHL

drugstore
farmacia
fahr-MAH-see-ah

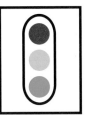

traffic lights
semáforo
seh-MAH-foe-roe

campsite
campamento
kahm-pah-MEHN-toe

telephone
teléfono
teh-LEH-foe-noe

bridge
puente
PWEHN-teh

city center
centro de la ciudad
SEHN-troe deh
lah see-oo-DAHD

restrooms
baños
BAH-nyoce

intersection
intersección
een-tehr-sek-see-OHN

post office
oficina de correo
oh-fee-SEE-nah
deh koh-RRE-oe

bus stop
parada del autobús
pah-RAH-dah dehl
aoo-toh-BOOS

curve
curva
KOOR-vah

At the café

To ask for something in a café, just name it and then say "please."

34 Excuse me.

Disculpe.

Dees-KOOL-peh.

35 What would you like?

¿Qué desea?

¿Keh deh-seh-AH?

36 A coffee, please.

Un café, por favor.

Oon kah-FEH, pohr fah-VOHR.

37 And an apple juice for me.

Y un jugo de manzana para mí.

EE oon HUH-goe deh mahn-ZAH-nah PAH-rah mee.

38 Right away.

Enseguida.

Ehn-seh-GEE-dah.

39 Do you have sandwiches?

¡Tienen sandwiches?

¡Tee-EH-nehn sandwiches?

40 Yes – ham and cheese.

Sí, de jamón y queso.

See, deh hah-MONE ee KEH-soe.

41 A ham sandwich, please.

Un sandwich de jamón, por favor.

Oon sandwich deh hah-MONE , pohr fah-VOHR.

42 Fine.

Bien.

Bee-EHN.

13

43 What kinds of ice cream do you have?

¿Qué clase de helado tiene?

¿Keh KLAH-seh deh eh-LAH-doe tee-EH-neh?

44 Vanilla, strawberry, and chocolate.

Vainilla, fresa y chocolate.

Va-ee-NEE-yah, FREH-sah ee choe-koe-LAH-teh.

45 A vanilla ice cream, please.

Un helado de vainilla, por favor.

Oon eh-LAH-doe deh va-ee-NEE-yah, pohr fah-VOHR.

46 And a lolli-pop for me.

Y un pirulí para mí.

Ee oon pee-ruh-LEE PAH-rah mee.

47 How much is it?

¿Cuánto es?

¿KWAHN-toe ehs?

48 Four pesetas, please.

Cuatro pesetas, por favor.

KWAH-troe peh-SEH-tahs, pohr fah-VOHR.

Word list

an orange juice
un jugo de naranja
*oon HUH-goe deh
nah-RAHN-hah*

a mineral water
un agua mineral
*oon AH-gwah
mee-neh-RAHL*

a lemonade
una limonada
*OO-nah lee-moh-
NAH-dah*

with ice
con hielo
kohn ee-EH-loe

a milk shake
una leche malteada
*OO-nah LEH-cheh
mahl-teh-AH-dah*

a cup of …
una taza de …
OO-nah TAH-zah deh …

a coffee with milk
un café con leche
*oon kah-FEH kohn
LEH-cheh*

a hot chocolate
un chocolate caliente
*oon choe-koe-LAH-teh
kah-lee-EHN-teh*

some sugar
un poco de azúcar
*oon POH-koe deh
ah-ZOO-kahr*

a pizza
una pizza
OO-nah PEE-zah

a hamburger
una hamburguesa
*OO-nah
ahm-bur-GAY-sah*

a grilled sandwich
un sandwich a la parrilla
*oon sandwich ah lah
pah-REE-yah*

some chips
unas papas fritas
*OO-nahs PAH-pahs
FREE-tahs*

a cake
un pastel
oon pahs-TEHL

15

At the restaurant

Here are the expressions that you will need to know when ordering in a restaurant.

49 A table for two, please.

Una mesa para dos, por favor.

OO-nah MEH-sah PAH-rah dose, pohr fah-VOHR.

50 The menu, please.

El menú, por favor.

Ehl meh-NOO, pohr fah-VOHR.

51 Are you ready?

¿Están listos?

¿Ehs-TAHN LEES-toce?

52 We'll have steak, please.

Queremos bistec, por favor.

Keh-REH-mohs bees-TEHK, pohr fah-VOHR.

53 For my main course, I'll have a pork chop.

De primer plato, quiero una chuleta de cerdo.

Deh pree-MEHR PLAH-toe, kee-EH-roe OO-nah choo-LEH-tah deh SEHR-doe.

54 And for dessert, an apple tart.

Y de postre, una tarta de manzana.

Ee deh POHS-treh, OO-nah TAHR-tah deh mahn-ZAH-nah.

55 And to drink?

¿Y para tomar?

¿Ee PAH-rah toh-MAHR?

56 What is this, please?

¿Qué es esto, por favor?

¿Keh ehs EHS-toe, pohr fah-VOHR?

57 More bread, please.

Más pan, por favor.

Mahs pahn, pohr fah-VOHR.

58 Are you finished?

¿Han terminado?

¿Ahn tehr-mee-NAH-doe?

59 The check, please.

La cuenta, por favor.

Lah KWEHN-tah, pohr fah-VOHR.

60 Is the tip included?

¿Está incluida la propina?

¿Ehs-TAH een-kloo-EE-dah lah proh-PEE-nah?

Word list

soup
sopa
SOE-pah

fish
pescado
pehs-KAH-doe

meat
carne
KAHR-neh

chicken
pollo
POH-yoe

vegetables
verduras
vehr-DOO-rahs

salad
ensalada
ehn-sah-LAH-dah

pasta
pasta
PAHS-tah

rice
arroz
ah-RROCE

fruit
fruta
FROO-tah

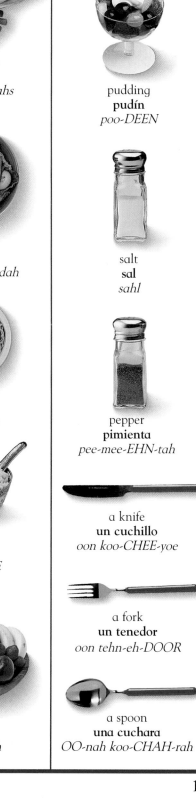

pudding
pudín
poo-DEEN

salt
sal
sahl

pepper
pimienta
pee-mee-EHN-tah

a knife
un cuchillo
oon koo-CHEE-yoe

a fork
un tenedor
oon tehn-eh-DOOR

a spoon
una cuchara
OO-nah koo-CHAH-rah

19

Shopping for food

Here and on the next page you can learn how to ask for things and find out how much they cost.

61 Four oranges.

Cuatro naranjas.

KWAH-troe nah-RAHN-hahs.

62 A kilo of apples, please.

Un kilo de manzanas, por favor.

Oon KEE-loe deh mahn-ZAH-nahs, pohr fah-VOHR.

63 How much is it?

¿Cuánto es?

¿KWAHN-toe ehs?

64 Ten pesetas fifty centavos.

Diez pesetas con cincuenta centavos.

Dee-EZ peh-SEH-tahs kohn seen-KWEHN-tah cehn-TAH-voce.

65
How much are the tomatoes?

66
Eight pesetas a kilo.

¿Cuánto cuestan los tomates?

Ocho pesetas el kilo.

¿KWAHN-toe KWEHS-tahn loce toh-MAH-tehs?

OH-choe peh-SEH-tahs ehl KEE-loe.

67
Do you have a bag, please?

68
Of course. Here you are.

¿Tiene una bolsa, por favor?

Por supuesto. Aquí la tiene.

¿Tee-EH-neh OO-nah BOHL-sah, pohr fah-VOHR?

Pohr soo-PWEHS-toe. Ah-KEE lah tee-EH-neh.

21

69 A piece of cheese, please.

Una tajada de queso, por favor.

OO-nah tah-HAH-dah deh KEH-soe, pohr fah-VOHR.

70 This much?

¿Así de grande?

¿Ah-SEE deh GRAN-deh?

71 A bit more.

Un poco más.

Oon POH-koe mahs.

72 That's fine.

Está bien.

Ehs-TAH bee-EHN.

73 Anything else?

¿Algo más?

¿AHL-goe mahs?

74 That's all. How much is it?

Eso es todo. ¿Cuánto es?

Eh-soe ehs TOH-doe. ¿KWAHN-toe ehs?

22

Word list

a loaf of bread
una barra de pan
*OO-nah BAH-rrah
deh pahn*

bread rolls
panecillos
pah-neh-SEE-yoce

butter
mantequilla
mahn-teh-KEE-yah

half a liter of milk
medio litro de leche
*MEH-dee-oh LEE-troe
deh LEH-cheh*

eggs
huevos
OOEH-voce

a jar of jam
un frasco de mermelada
*Oon FRAHS-koe deh
mehr-meh-LAH-dah*

cookies
galletas
gah-YEH-tahs

strawberries
fresas
FREH-sahs

bananas
bananos
bah-NAH-noce

grapes
uvas
OO-vahs

potatoes
papas
PAH-pahs

a bottle of ...
una botella de ...
*OO-nah boh-TEH-yah
deh...*

a can of ...
una lata de ...
OO-nah LAH-tah deh ...

a package of ...
una caja de ...
OO-nah KAH-hah deh ...

Shopping for clothes

These phrases are useful when you are shopping for clothes.

75 Can I help you?

¿En qué puedo servirle?

¿Ehn keh PWEH-doh sehr-VEER-leh?

76 I'm just looking, thank you.

Estoy mirando, no más, gracias.

Ehs-TOY mee-RAHN-doe, noe mahs, GRAH-see-ahs.

77 Do you have this sweater in blue?

¿Tiene este suéter en azul?

¿Tee-EH-neh EHS-teh SWEH-tehr ehn ah-ZOOL?

78 Yes. In blue, red, and yellow.

Sí. En azul, rojo y amarillo.

See. Ehn ah-ZOOL, ROH-hoe ee ah-mah-REE-yoe.

79 May I try it on?

¿Me lo puedo probar?

¿Meh loh PWEH-doe proh-BAHR?

80 Go ahead.

Por supuesto.

Pohr soo-PWEHS-toe.

81 I'll take this one.

Me llevaré éste.

Meh yeh-vah-REH EHS-teh.

82 That's 160 pesetas.

Son ciento sesenta pesetas.

Sohn see-EHN-toe seh-SEHN-tah peh-SEH-tahs.

25

Word list

T-shirt
camiseta
kah-mee-SEH-tah

shorts
pantalones cortos
*pahn-tah-LOE-nes
KOR-toce*

skirt
falda
FAHL-dah

pants
pantalones
pahn-tah-LOE-nes

sweatshirt
sudadera
sooh-dah-DEH-rah

dress
vestido
vehs-TEE-doe

shoes
zapatos
zah-PAH-toce

swimsuit
vestido de baño
*vehs-TEE-doe deh
BAH-nyoe*

sneakers
zapatos tenis
*zah-PAH-toce
TEH-nees*

cap
gorra
GOH-rrah

sunglasses
anteojos de sol
*ahn-teh-OH-hoce
deh sohl*

bag
bolsa
BOHL-sah

watch
reloj
reh-LOH

comb
peinilla
peh-ee-NEE-yah

brush
cepillo
seh-PEE-yoe

soap
jabón
hah-BONE

toothpaste
pasta dental
PAHS-tah dehn-TAHL

toothbrush
cepillo de dientes
seh-PEE-yoe deh dee-EHN-tehs

bandages
vendas
VEHN-dahs

postcard
tarjeta postal
tahr-HEH-tah pohs-TAHL

pencil
lápiz
LAH-peez

pen
estilográfica
ehs-tee-loe-GRAH-fee-kah

colored crayons
crayones de colores
krah-YOE-nehs deh koe-LOE-rehs

envelopes
sobres
SOE-brehs

paper
papel
pah-PEHL

camera
cámara
KAH-mah-rah

film
película
peh-LEE-koo-lah

book
libro
LEE-broh

ball
pelota
peh-LOE-tah

goggles
anteojos de natación
ahn-teh-OH-hoce deh nah-tah-SEE-ohn

boat
bote
BOE-teh

car
automóvil
aoo-toh-MOH-veel

doll
muñeca
moo-NYE-kah

Post offices and banks

Here you can find out how to ask for things in a post office or bank.

83 How much is a stamp for England?

¿Cuánto cuesta una estampilla para Inglaterra?

¡KWAHN-toe KWEHS-tah OO-nah ehs-tahm-PEE-yah PAH-rah Een-glah-TEH-rrah?

84 It's for a postcard.

Es para una postal.

Ehs PAH-rah OO-nah pohs-TAHL.

85 I'd like to send this letter to New York.

Me gustaría enviar esta carta a Nueva York.

Meh goos-tah-REE-ah ehn-VEE-ahr EHS-tah KAHR-tah ah Nweh-vah Yohrk.

86 I'd like to change some dollars.

Me gustaría cambiar dólares.

Meh goos-tah-REE-ah kahm-bee-AHR DOH-lah-rehs.

87 How much do you want to change?

¿Cuánto quiere cambiar?

¿KWAHN-toe KEE-eh-reh kahm-bee-AHR?

88 Fifty dollars, please.

Cincuenta dólares, por favor.

Seen-KWEHN-tah DOH-lah-rehs, pohr fah-VOHR.

Word list

a mailbox
un buzón
oon boo-ZOHN

travelers' checks
cheques viajeros
CHEH-kehs vee-ah-HEE-roce

a package
un paquete
oon pah-KEH-teh

by airmail
por correo aéreo
pohr koh-RREH-oh ah-EH-ree-oh

29

Sight-seeing

Use these phrases to ask for information
at a tourist office and places you visit.

89 Do you have
a street map?

¿Tiene
un mapa
de calles?

*¿Tee-EH-neh oon MAH-pah
deh KAH-yehs?*

90 Can you show
me on the map?

¿Puede indicarme
en el mapa?

*¿PWEH-deh een-dee-KAHR-meh
ehn ehl MAH-pah?*

91 When is the
museum open?

¿Cuándo abre el
museo?

*¿KWAHN-doe AH-breh
ehl moo-seh-OH?*

92 Every day, except
Tuesdays.

Todos los días,
menos los martes.

*TOH-doce loce DEE-ahs,
MEH-noce loce MAHR-tehs.*

93 How much is admission?

¿Cuánto cuesta la entrada?

¿KWAHN-toe KWEHS-tah lah ehn-TRAH-dah?

94 Two adults and a child, please.

Dos adultos y un niño, por favor.

Dose ah-DOOL-toce ee oon NEEN-yoe, pohr fah-VOHR.

95 I'd like a guidebook, please.

Deme una guía, por favor.

DEH-meh OO-nah GEE-ah, pohr fah-VOHR.

96 Can I take photos?

¿Puedo tomar fotos?

¿PWEH-doe toh-MAHR FOE-toce?

97 Are there guided tours?

¿Hay visitas guiadas?

¿AH-ee vee-SEE-tahs gee-AH-dahs?

98 When does the tour begin?

¿Cuándo empieza la visita?

¿KWAHN-doe ehm-pee-EH-zah lah vee-SEE-tah?

31

Word list

zoo
zoológico
zoh-oh-LOH-gee-koe

fair
feria
FEH-ree-ah

playground
lugar de recreo
*loo-GAHR deh
reh-KREH-oh*

boat trip
viaje en bote
*vee-AH-heh ehn
BOE-teh*

sports arena
estadio
ehs-TAH-dee-oh

circus
circo
SEER-koe

movie theater
cine
SEE-neh

theater
teatro
teh-AH-troe

art gallery
galería de arte
*gah-leh-REE-ah deh
AHR-teh*

church
iglesia
ee-GLEH-see-ah

lake
lago
LAH-goe

beach
playa
PLAH-yah

mountains
montañas
mohn-TAH-nyahs

harbor
puerto
PWEHR-toe

farm
granja
GRAHN-hah

Danger!
¡Peligro!
¡Peh-LEE-groe!

No swimming.
Prohibido nadar.
*Proh-ee-BEE-doe
nah-DAHR.*

Beware of the dog.
Cuidado con el perro.
*koo-ee-DAH-doe kohn
ehl PEH-rroe.*

Do not touch.
No tocar.
Noe toh-KAHR.

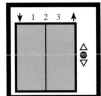

elevator
elevador
eh-leh-vah-DOOR

stairs
escaleras
ehs-kah-LEH-rahs

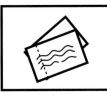

tickets
boletos
boh-LEH-toce

Open
Abierto
Ah-bee-EHR-toe

Closed
Cerrado
Seh-RRAH-doe

Way out/Exit
Salida
Sah-LEE-dah

You are here.
Usted está aquí.
*Oos-TEHD ehs-TAH
ah-KEE.*

Entrance
Entrada
ehn-TRAH-dah

Emergency exit
Salida de emergencia
*Sah-LEE-dah deh
eh-mehr-GEHN-cee-ah*

No entry.
Prohibida la entrada
*Proh-ee-BEE-dah lah
ehn-TRAH-dah*

Opening hours
**Horario de atención al
público**
*Oh-RAH-ree-oh deh
ah-tehn-see-OHN ahl
POO-blee-koh*

Admission free
Entrada gratis
*Ehn-trah-dah
GRAH-tees*

Cashier
Cajero
Kah-HEH-roe

At the hotel

These phrases will help you ask for information in a hotel and reserve a room.

99 Could I have a room?

¿Me puede dar una habitación?

¿Meh PWEH-deh dahr OO-nah ah-bee-tah-see-OHN?

100 For how many people?

¿Para cuántas personas?

¿PAH-rah KWAHN-tahs pehr-SOE-nahs?

101 For two adults and one child.

Para dos adultos y un niño.

PAH-rah dose ah-DOOL-toce ee uhn NEEN-yoe.

102 A room with a private bathroom?

¿Una habitación con baño privado?

¿OO-nah ah-bee-tah-see-OHN kohn bah-NYOE pree-VAH-doe?

103 How many nights are you staying?

¿Cuántas noches va a quedarse?

¿KWAHN-tahs NOE-chehs vah ah keh-DAHR-seh?

104 Two nights.

Dos noches.

Dose NOE-chehs.

105 Is breakfast included?

¿Está incluido el desayuno?

¿Ehs-TAH een-kloo-EE-doe ehl deh-sah-YOO-noe?

106 It's room number five.

Es la habitación número cinco.

Ehs lah ah-bee-tah-see-OHN NOO-meh-roe SEEN-koe.

107 Here's your key.

Aquí tiene su llave.

Ah-KEE tee-EH-neh soo YAH-veh.

Making friends

Use these phrases to tell new friends something about yourself.

108 What's your name?

¿Cómo te llamas?

¿KOE-moe teh YAH-mahs?

109 My name is Emma.

Me llamo Emma.

Meh YAH-moe EH-mmah.

110 How old are you?

¿Cuántos años tienes?

¿KWAHN-toce AN-yoce tee-EH-nehs?

111 I am eight.

Tengo ocho.

TEHN-goe OH-choe.

112 Where are you from?

¿De dónde eres?

¿Deh DOHN-deh EH-rehs?

113 I'm from Chicago.

Soy de Chicago.

Soy deh Chicago.

114 Are you on vacation?

¿Estás de vacaciones?

¿Ehs-TAHS deh vah-kah-see-OH-nehs?

115 Yes, with my family.

Sí, con mi familia.

See, kohn mee fah-MEE-lee-ah.

116 Do you have any brothers and sisters?

¿Tienes hermanos y hermanas?

¿Tee-EH-nehs ehr-MAH-noce ee ehr-MAH-nahs?

117 I have one brother.

Tengo un hermano.

TEHN-goe oon ehr-MAH-noe.

At the station

You will use these phrases if you buy tickets or ask for information at a railroad station.

118 One ticket for Madrid, please.

Un boleto para Madrid, por favor.

Oon boh-LEH-toe PAH-rah Mah-DREED, pohr fah-VOHR.

119 One-way?

¿De una sola vía?

¿Deh OO-nah SOH-lah VEE-ah?

120 No. Round trip.

No. De ida y vuelta.

Noe. Deh EE-dah ee VOO-ehl-tah.

121 A schedule, please.

Un horario, por favor.

Oon oh-RAH-ree-oh, pohr fah-VOHR.

122 What time is the next train to Madrid?

¿A qué hora sale el próximo tren para Madrid?

¿Ah keh OH-rah SAH-leh ehl PROHK-see-moe trehn PAH-rah Mah-DREED?

123 Which track does the Madrid train leave from?

¿De qué plataforma sale el tren para Madrid?

¿Deh keh plah-tah-FOHR-mah SAH-leh ehl trehn PAH-rah Mah-DREED?

124 From track four.

De la plataforma cuatro.

Deh lah plah-tah-FOHR-mah KWAH-troe.

125 Is this the Madrid train?

¿Es éste el tren para Madrid?

¿Ehs EHS-teh ehl trehn PAH-rah Mah-DREED?

126 Yes. Change at Toledo.

Sí. Cambie en Toledo.

See. KAHM-bee-eh ehn Toh-LEH-doe.

Telling the time

Here you can find out how to ask and tell the time. Turn to page 42 to learn more numbers.

127 What time is it?

¿Qué hora es?

¿Keh OH-rah ehs?

128 It's one o'clock.

Es la una.

Ehs la OO-nah.

129

two o'clock
dos en punto
dose ehn POON-toe

130

five after two
dos y cinco
dose ee SEEN-koh

131

quarter after two
dos y cuarto
dose ee KWAHR-toe

132

half past two
dos y media
dose ee MEH-dee-ah

133

quarter to three
un cuarto para las tres
*oon KWAHR-toe
PAH-rah lahs trehs*

134

five to three
cinco para las tres
*SEEN-koh PAH-rah
lahs trehs*

135

in the morning
en la mañana
ehn lah mah-NYAH-nah

136

in the afternoon
en la tarde
ehn lah TAHR-deh

137

in the evening
en la noche
ehn lah NOE-cheh

138

at midday
al mediodía
*ahl meh-dee-oh-
DEE-ah*

139

at midnight
a la medianoche
*ah lah meh-dee-ah-
NOE-cheh*

140

in half an hour
en media hora
ehn MEH-dee-ah OH-rah

Numbers

1
uno
OO-noe

2
dos
dose

3
tres
trehs

cuatro
KWAH-troe

5
cinco
SEEN-koe

seis
SEH-ees

siete
see-EH-teh

8
ocho
OH-choe

nueve
noo-EH-veh

10
diez
dee-EZ

11
once
OHN-seh

doce
DOE-seh

13
trece
TREH-seh

catorce
kah-TOHR-seh

15
quince
KEEN-seh

dieciséis
dee-eh-see-SEH-ees

17
diecisiete
dee-eh-see-see-EH-teh

18
dieciocho
dee-eh-see-OH-choe

diecinueve
dee-eh-see-noo-EH-veh

20
veinte
veh-EEN-teh

21
veintiuno
veh-een-tee-OO-noe

22
veintidós
veh-een-tee-DOSE

veintitrés
veh-een-tee-TREHS

24
veintcuatro
veh-een-tee-KWAH-troe

veinticinco
veh-een-tee-SEEN-koe

veintiséis
veh-een-tee-SEH-ees

27
veintisiete
veh-een-tee-see-EH-teh

veintiocho
veh-een-tee-OH-choe

29
veintinueve
veh-een-tee-noo-EH-veh

treinta
treh-EEN-tah

cuarenta
kwah-ah-REHN-tah

50
cincuenta
seen-KWEHN-tah

42

60
sesenta
seh-SEHN-tah

70
setenta
seh-TEHN-tah

80
ochenta
oh-CHEN-tah

90
noventa
noh-VEHN-tah

100
cien
SEE-ehn

Colors

red
rojo
ROH-hoe

yellow
amarillo
ah-mah-REE-yoe

blue
azul
ah-ZOOL

green
verde
VEHR-deh

purple
púrpura
POOR-poo-rah

orange
naranja
nah-RAHN-hah

brown
marrón
mah-RROHN

white
blanco
BLAHN-koe

black
negro
NEH-groe

Days

Monday
lunes
LOO-nehs

Tuesday
martes
MAHR-tehs

Wednesday
miércoles
mee-EHR-koh-lehs

Thursday
jueves
hoo-EH-vehs

Friday
viernes
vee-EHR-nehs

Saturday
sábado
SAH-bah-doe

Sunday
domingo
doh-MEEN-goe

week
semana
seh-MAH-nah

weekend
fin de semana
feen deh seh-MAH-nah

43

Help!

These phrases are useful when you need help, have hurt yourself, or feel sick.

141 Can you help me?

¿Puede ayudarme?

¿PWEH-deh ah-yoo-DAHR-meh?

142 I'm lost.

Estoy perdido.

Ehs-TOY pehr-DEE-doe.

143 I've lost my passport.

He perdido mi pasaporte.

Eh pehr-DEE-doe mee pah-sah-POHR-teh.

144 My wallet has been stolen.

Me han robado la billetera.

Meh ahn roh-BAH-doe lah bee-yeh-TEH-rah.

145 My camera isn't working.

Mi cámara no funciona.

Mee KAH-mah-rae noe foon-see-OH-nah.

146 Help!

¡Auxilio!

¡Ah-oohk-SEE-lee-oh!

147 There's been an accident.

Ha ocurrido un accidente.

Ah oh-kuh-REE-doe uhn ahk-see-DEHN-teh.

148 I've cut myself.

Me he cortado.

Meh eh kohr-TAH-doe.

149 I don't feel well.

No me siento bien.

Noe meh see-EHN-toe bee-EHN.

150 Where does it hurt?

¿Dónde te duele?

¿DOHN-deh teh doo-EH-leh?

English index

In each index, only one page reference is given for each word or phrase, unless a word or phrase has more than one translation.

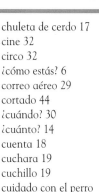

Spanish index